Martial Arts
History, Forms and Techniques
Volume One

Pan Gai Noon
Kung Fu to Karate

by
Al Case

Quality Press

Copyright © 2024 by Alton H. Case

For information regarding this book go to:

MonsterMartialArts.com

AlCaseBooks.com

TABLE OF CONTENTS

SANCHIN

SEISAN

Part One
SANCHIN

introduction
FORMS ARE THE HEART OF THE ART.

Within a form you will find perfect theory; the techniques of the form will enable you to bring that perfect theory into reality; and freestyle will enable you to further translate that theory into the chaos of out and out combat.

But, without matrixing, the forms are nothing but random tricks and out of alignment sequences. Indeed, to study the forms without understanding Matrixing is like mixing the numbers from 1 to 100 in a hat...and then trying to draw them out in order.

Matrixing aligns the data, presents all the data, enables you to understand the art in such a way that there can be no confusion. Imagine, fighting without confusion. Why...it would be like not fighting at all. There would never be any guesswork, and you would always know what to do.

Still, you have to have the basic data first, and the basic data, no matter what mish mashed arrangement it is in, is in the forms.

CHAPTER ONE
THE POWER OF KARATE!

One day I noticed something funny at my gym. There was one fellow who was always at one particular piece of machinery. He rarely worked on other equipment, and I began to wonder what, exactly, his training regimen was. "Say, what kind of a routine do you practice?" I had set myself up on the machine next to him and I broached the subject as he came off his work out.

"Biceps," he said. He grinned and flexed his arm. Sure enough, his biceps was a darned cannonball. "Anything else?" He had a build that was solid, but not spectacular. "Nah," he replied. He indicated his muscle. "This is the Power! This is the punch! This is the whole point of it all!" And he made a shadow boxing motion from his sitting position.

Perhaps you know where I am going with this? What is True Power? And how does power relate to the Martial Arts? Before I go on I recommend you look up such words as Power, Strength and Force in the dictionary. Highly enlightening reading.

So what is Power? The ability to make something happen. And this young man with the enlarged biceps had an incorrect idea of what Power was.

Think about it. He referred to his biceps as the power of the punch. But the fact of the matter is that a punch relies not on the tightening of the biceps, but of the muscles on the back of the arm! And, in fact, it is conceivable that an overly tight biceps could slow down a punch! Hmmm. So, let's talk about developing Power.

Power, in the Martial Arts, is commonly understood as the ability to deliver Force. In common parlance this means, if you'll pardon the phrasing, "How hard ya can hit the sucka!" But if you want to be more than a Popeye, you'll have do delve a little deeper.

$$\text{Mass x Velocity} = \text{Force}$$

Now we're talking!

And, translating these physics into the Martial Arts world, 'How hard ya can hit the sucka' depends upon how much weight you can overload his frame with.

So a guy builds up a triceps, not a biceps, and it weighs more, and it can go faster, therefore he can hit harder.

Well, yes, but it's not very effective. And the reason it is not very effective is because an arm weighs maybe 10-20 pounds? And 10-20 pounds, even in the face, is not enough to damage an opponent to any real extent.

So, how do we develop real power? How do we develop that fabulous 'One Punch Knock Out Power' that Karate is famous for? That's easy. Hit with your whole body. That's right, instead of swinging an arm, you must propel your entire weight into an opponent. This concept, referred to by some as 'Using the body as one unit,' is the point of effective, classical Karate.

Imagine, if you will, an opponent lying on the ground. Now, drop a bag of sand, approximately your weight, and with a two by four extending out of it, onto that opponent.

Can you see it? Can you imagine what would happen?

Now multiply that force with as much downward push as you can muster, and you will have the idea of what is behind a real punch. So, let's talk about the place muscles have in this concept.

Muscles are necessary for starting the whole body in motion, then they must immediately relax. The reason they must relax is because that which is loose is faster than that which is tight.

And the muscles must tighten upon impact. The reason they must tighten at this point is because the frame must be solid enough to withstand the impact of your body weight, times velocity, upon an opponent.

Go into freefall from a six foot fence. Assume the prone and catch yourself in a push up position. That is the force your arms must be able to accept if you are going to put your whole weight into a punch.

Then the muscles will tighten to retract. Retracting is important because if you don't retract then the impact of the strike will go back your own arm. But if you take the arm away then the force is left in the opponent!

Finally, relax inbetween the retraction, and then tighten the muscles momentarily to stop them in a position deemed admirable for follow up.

So you start the body with muscles. (Launch body weight) You stop the body with muscles. (Assume final striking position with weapon inside opponent's body) You start the body again. (Retract weapon to leave max impact and to not leave yourself open to counter) And you stop the body again. (Assume new attacking position)

Start, stop, start, stop. (Additional Hint: Breath out when the body expands, breath in when it contracts.) And now, perhaps, you understand why some Arts propose circular action as more efficient. There are less startings and stoppings in a circle. However, an arc can be less efficient than a straight line, so there will be balancings between these concepts of Arts.

So how do you achieve maximum efficiency in Karate? Well, when doing the Forms you should analyze which muscle is being used when. For instance, in a back stance the rear leg should be turned more forward than it commonly is. The reason is because if your rear foot is turned sideways it 1) splits the intention between two stances (Horse and Rear) and 2) doesn't utilize the large front muscle on the leg properly, or the best angle for traction in the foot.

And this concept of aligning the muscles for proper usage must be examined through every move of every form, while taking into account all self defenses and their deviations. And it must be done so thoroughly that the knowledge becomes intuitive. And that is why the old Masters admonished their students to practice their Forms, to even spend their whole lifetimes on Forms.

So, let's look a little deeper. Just turning the muscle so it is on the proper side of the limb is not enough. The limb itself must be at the proper angle for the job to be done. Stand with the Tan Tien outside the base of the feet and you can be uprooted (shoved over). Stand with the back leaning improper to the stance and you can be pushed or pulled over. Stand with the arms too bent and they can be collapsed. Stand with the arms too extended and they can be used for levers. And so on. (Additional hint: Line up the limbs of the body with the Tan Tien.)

The fact of the matter is that a muscle has an optimum working range. For the elbow, that being the simplest to explore, the best working range is between 90 and 135 degrees. Too little and the block collapses. Too much and the block misses.

To check this out simply stand in a stance and do an Outward Block (fist level to the shoulder). Have somebody push on that block. They should push directly back towards your body. If your arm is less than 90 degrees it will be weaker, if it is more than 135 degrees then you are exposing surface for an attack, and giving your opponent a lever.

Try this exercise with your stances, with your blocks and strikes. If you fall over from push or pull then you probably have a wrong skeletal angle, and thus your structure will collapse. So how can you punch or block effectively if your structure collapses under a mere push or pull? What is going to happen when that push or pull becomes a punch or a throw? The conclusion is that muscles must be examined, and the skeletal structure must be aligned, before one can attain any degree of proficiency in the Martial Arts. Again, the study of Forms is advised to plumb these matters.

Let's consider one more item in this matter of developing power. Timing.

As has been intimated earlier in this article, the body must move as one unit. Simply, all of the weight must land on the opponent at one time. The easiest way to understand this is to go through your Forms slowly, a la Tai Chi, and to synchronize the motions of the body. The hand and the foot must synchronize. The knee and the elbow must synchronize. The shoulder and the hip must synchronize. And, to re-emphasize, all must start at the same moment, and all must stop (land) at the same moment.

So, let's draw a few conclusions from all the data I've given you in this article.

First, muscles are fine. I won't denigrate body building, it is too valuable. But a person who thinks a biceps is a punch is confusing image with reality.

Second, one should understand that Karate is in the Forms. The Forms are a blueprint for body motion, and that blue print must be studied scientifically, much the same way an architect studies a building plan. All tolerances must be accounted for, and all potential motions must be accounted for.

Incidentally, what many people don't seem to realize is that Karate Forms are calisthenics. They are muscle builders, and they build the muscles exactly the way they are supposed to be built, and in the right proportion, for the task one is preparing oneself for.

Third, one should realize a simple fact. Power is not your weight. Power is not your size. Power is not how much you can lift. Power is not your muscles. Power is your knowledge. Even a child, with the correct knowledge, is capable of learning the Power of Karate. And a man without knowledge is weaker than the weakest child.

CHAPTER TWO
DEVELOPING INTERNAL ENERGY IN KARATE

'The Old Master threw his attacker to the roof with a mere touch!' Or, 'The Old Master slapped the horse on the rump and the horse died!' No doubt you have heard these and many other stories of the application of mystical powers. Every Art has them. The purpose of this article is to present certain methods by which a practitioner of Karate can develop Internal Power. Before proceeding there are certain factors that must be included in every practitioner's training before the following exercises will work.

CBM

The student must CBM. CBM means 'Coordinated Body Motion,' and it means that all parts of the body support one intention. This means that hands and feet move in conjunction with each other to support one intention. It means that breathing is coordinated with body motion. It means one must sink their weight and align their structure when doing technique. It means focusing of body and Energies until the Intention of the human being begins to manifest.

The best way of CBMing is to realize the points of the above paragraph in conjunction with classical Form. Simply, go through each Form concentrating on each of the elements listed above in turn. A student will definitely CBM using this method. To be honest, the student who attempts the following exercises without CBMing will experience consider lack of success.

FIRE

The fire being spoken of here is a candle. Simply stand in front of a candle elevated to a comfortable height (depending upon what stance you are working from) and punch. When punching lock the fist one inch in front of the candle. Do not retract for a few seconds. Do not punch the candle again until the flame has 'Settled.'

This is a simple exercise which everyone knows. However, as simple as it is nobody ever takes it as far as it needs to go. People will punch the candle for an hour or two over a week or two, attain some success, and then say, 'What's the big deal?'

The 'Big deal' is not measured in a short time. The 'Big deal is measured over a couple of hundred hours in a couple of years. What will happen is that you will overcome the need for power in the Punch. You will find that you need less and less power to put out the candle. Eventually your punch will be as light as a feather, yet the candle will go out consistently and easily. This is because you will be punching with Intention (Ki) instead of muscle.

A word of advice, start with one candle for each hand. Practice for a week, then add a candle. Eventually you will be counting your progress by how many candles you can put out in an hour.

Once you have achieved some degree of success you may increase the distance between the candle and the punch. Remember, the essence of this technique is in relaxing the body between strikes, and relaxing the mind at all times.

A word of caution. As with anything, this can be overdone. While the chances are small, if you do become sick from this simply stop for a week or two and start again from one candle. In otherwords, take your time, don't overstress your body, and realize that success is measured in patience.

WATER

Karate is, predominately, strikes and blocks. There is not much evasion in the classical study of Karate, though only a fool would ignore the subject of evasion, especially when considering that the fellow who tries to mug you will be bigger, stronger, have friends, have weapons, and so on.

To develop Internal Power in your blocks is incredibly easy. Simply dip your hands in a bucket of water and practice your blocks. When you block you must flick the hand so that the water flies off. In otherwords, block until your hands are dry, then do it again and again and again.

This is fun because you don't have to lock yourself into one stance or mode of movement for extended lengths of time, such as you would when striking a candle. Instead, you can practice your forms, working your blocks in a variety of ways, and explore the variety of Karate while plumbing the depths.

The idea here is to 'Flick Energy.' When you flick water you are practicing the simple fact of focus to the extreme, and you are creating, exactly, the concept of flicking Energy (Ki) from your hands.

Again, as in the candle exercise, start with a few minutes, maybe one dipping of hands, and work up until you have to dip your hands again and again and again for an hour.

And, again, if you get sick, realize that the body sometimes has to get used to the moving of wholesale amounts of Energy through it, and take a week off before starting all over again.

The study of Karate, to be honest, is so straightforward that it is highly unlikely that you would suffer any kind of internal injury from the practices outlined in this article.

EARTH

Earth refers to Stances. Stances are incredibly important to any Art. Stance creates the connection between the body and the planet, and thus an interchange of Energy can occur. If you don't believe this then simply settle for the explanation that a machine must be bolted down to function at its most efficient.

Gichin Funakoshi, who you may have heard of, liked to practice his stance by standing on a roof holding a tatami mat in the middle of a hurricane.

Now that's intense!

The easier way, or at least the lesser method which will lead you to more intense methods, is to create Internal Energy in your stance by having somebody push on your body when you are practicing. They must push correctly, so as to help you find the correct alignment between the limb and the Tan Tien and the ground.

This is called 'Body Testing,' and at first the student will simply push back. After a short while, however, the student will relax and begin to concentrate with his mind, and become aware of the energetical connections within his body. Eventually, through continued practice, the student will give up pushing back entirely and realize that his Energy is channelable, directable, usable, and so on. At this point 'Grounding' the body will become so easy that it is a fact of relaxed thought, instead of a struggle. Actually, once a person understands this principle they will have no problem Grounding while in a one legged stance (Crane Stance).

Incidentally, this exercise will result in a degree of 'Iron body' without the need for any esoteric practices. Since this section deals with stance, and because proper stance is so crucial to the development of Classical Karate, there are a couple of other items that should be considered.

Specific Forms can be practiced to aid in your stancing. This is helpful if you don't have somebody to press on your structure, or if you want to concentrate on certain stances.

The Form Sanchin is excellent for developing Grounding through the Hourglass Stance.

The Tekki forms are excellent for the Horse Stance.

There is also a method called (in Korean) 'Kima Chasie,' which means 'Horse Meditation.' When doing Kima Chasie one simply stays in a Horse Stance with one hand raised in a high block and the other hand to the side in a rearward 'Beak.' The idea is to stare at the tips of the fingers in the beak until one 'Forgets,' or otherwise mentally deals with the pain. Concentrating the breathing to the Tan Tien helps immensely in this exercise.

AIR

This, and the following item, are not methods, so much as data necessary to make the previous methods work. If you take this data to heart then you will find other methods, relating to the three presented here, on your own.

Air has to do with Intention.

In the beginning of this article the concept of CBM was outlined. As the student progresses through the exercises in this article he will realize that breathing is one of the most important elements of CBM. Correct breathing allows one to pursue the deeper meanings of Karate.

Blocks become sensations, rather than hard effort. Striking becomes like 'Breathing' an attacker away.

The correct way of breathing is: Breath out when the body expands. Breath in when the body contracts. Breath out when doing a technique. Breath out when being struck.

Breathing aids relaxation, and relaxation allows perception, and no technique can be mastered without perception. If you doubt this then consider how much Art there can be without perception.

VOID

'Void,' being the essence of Karate and the Martial Arts, means to be totally perceptive. Not to fill the space around yourself with useless mental chatter and inner conversations, but to be 'Still' in your thought process, and thus give yourself the chance to listen to and perceive what is going on around you. For example, when a person attacks you there will be a wave of Energy that is meant to overwhelm you and frighten you into the motionlessness of a good target/victim. Only by keeping your senses open, and not 'Buying' the wave of attacking Energy, can you manage to withstand the attack coinciding with, or right behind the wave of Energy. And the way to do this is to practice the Art until you are 'Void' of mental activity that would interfere with your analyzing and handling the intended Force/Flow. This principle can be applied to all Martial Arts.

CONCLUSION

To understand fully what the essence of this article is about one should consider the words of Yasutsune Itosu who, in 1908, said, 'One to two hours of hard training every day for three or four years will make you master Karate.'

Nowadays it is three or four years to Black Belt and ten to twelve years to mastery.

What happened? Why does it take longer? The reason it takes longer is because people get away from the intensity of training outlined here, and start practicing for other purposes. They want to win the tournament, or they get involved in crossing Arts without really understanding what they are doing, or they can't make a technique work so they change it, instead of investing the time necessary to make it work, or their system has become top heavy with instruction and additions.

The truth is if you want to Master Karate, to the degree that practitioners of old did, simply divide your time between candles, blocks, and then applying the techniques to a partner. The question is, are you intense enough to do it?

CHAPTER THREE
THE THREE CONCEPTS OF SANCHIN
'If you don't know Sanchin...you don't know Karate.'

I had been in the Martial Arts for over two decades before I heard this old saying. Now I love Karate. And I had practiced the traditional forms until they came out my ears. In fact, I had done so much Karate I had...moved on.

But I heard this phrase and felt an immediate jolt to the nervous system.

So I went out and purchased the book by George Mattson, and ordered videos concerning Sanchin, and I found that not only was my interest in Karate revitalized, my study of the Arts was enhanced in a way that has not only refused to wane, but has been growing in a manner which I never expected.

Sanchin means 'Three battles,' or, 'Three conflicts. While some hold that this refers to 'body, mind and spirit,' it sounds a little too 'Western.' And I have heard the theory that there are three techniques in Sanchin, 13 techniques in Seisan, and 36 techniques in Sanseirui. This is the literal meaning of the names of the 3 original forms of Pan Gai Noon (half hard/half soft), the Chinese Art which became the Okinawan Art of Uechi-Ryu.

However, while one could cull the forms for specific techniques and order techniques in the numerical manner I have just described, I don't think that three techniques are the essence of Sanchin. It is my theory that Sanchin refers, actually, to 'Three concepts.'

The three concepts are: Thrusting, as defined by the double spear thrusts occurring twice within the form. Specifically, there are the opening downward thrusting motion, and there are the three upward (towards the opponent's head) thrusting motions.

Horizontal Circular Motion, as defined by the 'Pot holding and inward circle to eye thrust motion which occurs in the main bulk of the form (while walking forward, turning and walking back, and walking forward again).

Vertical Circular Motion, as defined by the last three 'Tiger' moves of the form.

These three concepts make a very solid and complete platform for an Art. Specifically, the Horizontal and Vertical circles describe a sphere which can be held in the hands, and which can absorb virtually any attack. The Thrusting, of course, is the return Flow to an attack.

THRUSTING

When I teach my students how to thrust I point out that the arms must be arranged so that the Energy of the Tan Tien can align with the finished product, and that somewhere between the retraction of the arms (prior to thrust) and the thrusting, there must exist a bend in the arms which will result in a 'Waving,' or 'Pulsing' of energy.

This concept is actually visible in virtually any strike, and is inherent within the system. In practicing traditional Karate styles (Shotokan types) it took me a dozen years to pulse Energy through a strike. But in practicing Sanchin I found that the 'Pulsing' occurred more naturally, and had more potential for evolution.

Pulsing aside, the application of this concept is incredibly sweet and natural. I describe the application as 'Overriding.' When somebody strikes at you simply strike at the same time and utilize the strike as a block and Override them. Go through their arms. Make a slight shift to gain the superior angle (inside or out) and develop resolution and intention that will reign supreme. This concept is simple, and can be applied to any strike, and there is no end to the exercises you can develop to further this concept.

HORIZONTAL CIRCULAR MOTION

One is 'Holding a thousand pound pot,' and walking while thrusting. The motion is horizontal and the arm comes across in an Inward Block with the edge of the hand, circles and Thrusts with a pulse.

I have to be honest, I disagree with the way virtually every practitioner of Sanchin proposes the Form.

The common practice is to bring the hand in, withdraw it, and thrust it. This involves several starts and stops of the muscles.

I believe the correct way to do this maneuver, the way that puts more emphasis on 'Pulsing' and less on muscle, is to make a circle of the hand and eliminate the starting and stopping.

Starting and stopping takes time, is not efficient, and destroys the Pulsing effect of the strike. The circular motion I propose has only one start and stop, defines the Pulse, and is much more efficient.

Interestingly, I am probably prone to this theory because of exposure to 'The Unbendable Arm of Aikido, and the fact that I use the Unbendable Arm with a 'Pulse' in Pa Kua extensively.

VERTICAL CIRCULAR MOTION

The vertical motion is described by the last three moves of the Form. I suggest pointing the fingers and Pulsing the palm in the initial Low Block of the move. After this Low Block the hands circle in a vertical fashion, utilizing the Circular Block of Pan Gai Noon.

Practice the Form for any length of time and the student will realize that the Circular Block is the real essence of the Form, and of the Art.

In Uechi-Ryu this block is called 'Wa-uke,' and it absorbs, deflects, traps, and opens the door to an incredible variety of response. If one wishes to examine that variety one should actually learn Seisan.

Sanchin, while opening the door to the basic concepts and techniques, is a Form of Power. It is strength. It is Energy.

Seisan is a Form of technique. Sanchin is taught first so that a student will have the proper strength to make the techniques work.

In China a student was made to wash floors and provide other simple tasks until the teacher decided he had the proper mental attitude to learn the Art.

The first three months of real instruction, when it finally ocurred, the student did only the opening Thrusting motions of the Form. That was all.

Stand in one place and thrust for a couple of hours. Come back the next day and do the same thing. Day after day. Month after month.

In such slow fashion was Sanchin taught, the student taking three years to learn the simplicities involved. Yet the student that was taught in this fashion was strong, powerful and able. And it was taught that it took ten years to really learn the Form.

At this point let me outline some of the things a good instructor will look for when teaching Sanchin.

The feet should be turned in so as to grip the ground or brace. The knees should be turned in. Not only does this help the 'Bracing' of the stance upon the ground, but allows for excellent 'Kick Catching' techniques.

The hips should be thrust forward, which will strengthen the small of the back.

The small of the back should be firm, as if resisting a pushing palm.

The line of the shoulders should be over the line of the hips should be over the line of the feet.

The shoulders should be held low. If they are up the arms can be lifted and the whole body uprooted.

The elbows should be kept tight to protect, and to conserve the line of Energy to the Tan Tien.

The wrists should be straight, like an iron rod, unless the student is Pulsing Energy in a strike or block.

Pulsing Energy should be performed with the arms until the whole body learns how to Pulse Energy.

Breathing should be done to the Tan Tien and the body should be sunk into the ground with total intention. The Instructor can test this concept by Body Testing and seeing all his Energies transmitted through the student's form into the ground.

As the student progresses pushes can become strikes, gaining in severity, and the student should make serious inroads into the concept of an 'Iron Body.'

Breathing, while often precisely defined, should be from and to the Tan Tien. The serious students spends much time examining the various depths of breathing to understand how to keep the body hard and yet mobile while practicing Sanchin.

In conclusion let me say that Sanchin is a wonderful exercise. But the wonder comes not from mysterious techniques, but rather from the depth of training undertaken. I had years of Martial Training, I had a catalog of techniques that had much breadth. I had studied different Arts and thought I knew...a lot. But, relatively speaking, I was lacking in depth.

Depth is the spirit. Depth is how deep you go into something...and into yourself.

Breadth is how many techniques you know, and breadth doesn't require an enhanced ability to move and ground and Focus and Pulse and...Depth does.

Posing or ability? Fancy moves or...accomplishments? Sanchin is the difference.

CHAPTER FOUR
SANCHIN

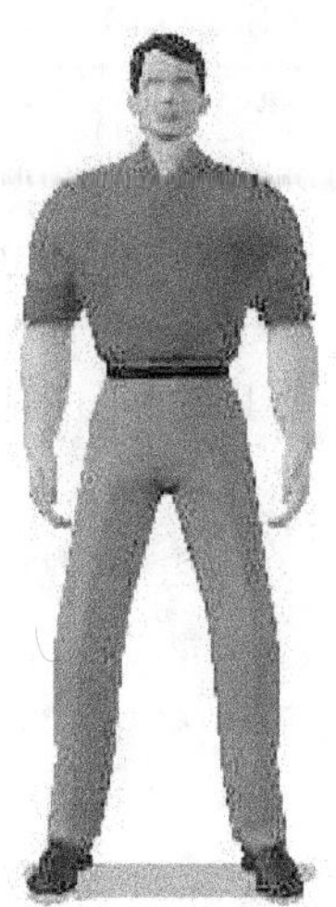

Starting position: relaxed, but ready to move in any direction quickly and easily.

1a)   Right half-moon step as you draw the hands upward (as if drawing pistols). Assume an hourglass stance as you spear downward with both hands.

1b)   Close the fists and cross them, then raise them.

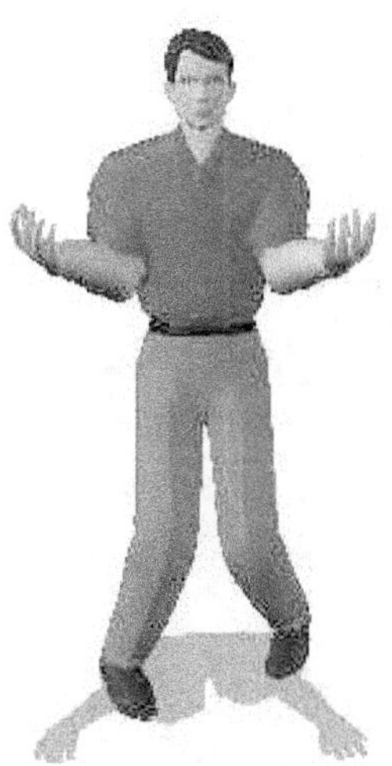

Open the arms and open the hands. Imagine yourself as holding a thousand pound pot.

1c)   Bring the left hand inward and backward in circlular motion.

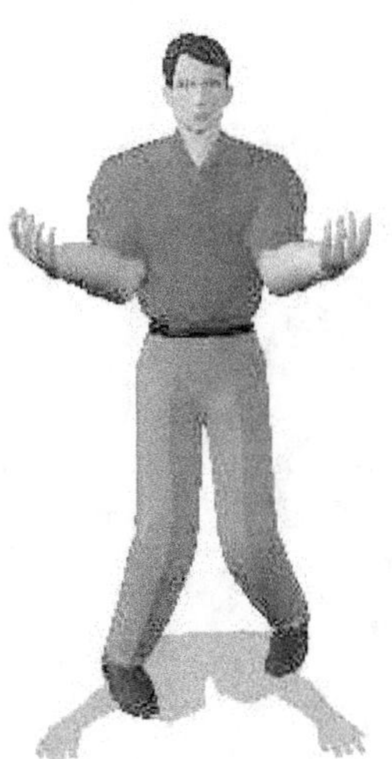

Left spear thrust. The thrust is not fully extended, but between a curve and a thrust, as if being used to override a strike. Retract the left hand to the double outward (pot holding position) arm position.

2a)   Left half-moon step into an hourglass stance.

2b)   Circle the right arm inward and outward and execute a right, semi-extended spear thrust.

Retract the left hand to the double outward (pot holding position) arm position.

3a)   Right half-moon step into an hourglass stance

3b)   Bring the left hand   inward and backward in a circular movement.

Left, semi-circular spear thrust. Retract the left hand to the double outward (pot holding position) arm position.

4a)   Right foot steps over the left foot in a dragon step. Pivot to an hourglass stance facing to the rear.

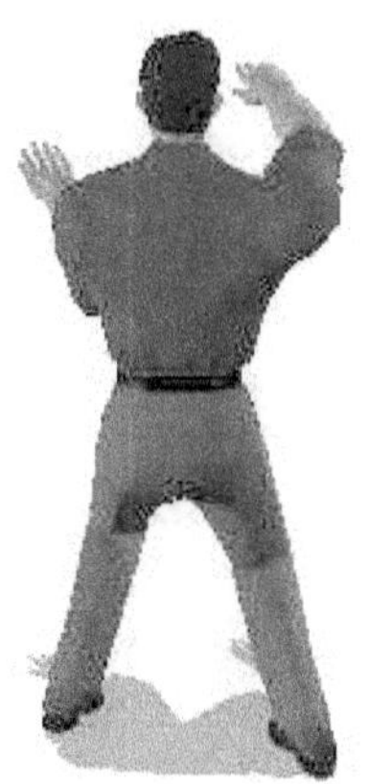

4b)   Execute a right semi-circular spear thrust. Retract.

5a)   Right half-moon step into an hourglass stance.

5b)   Execute a left, semi-circular spear thrust. Retract.

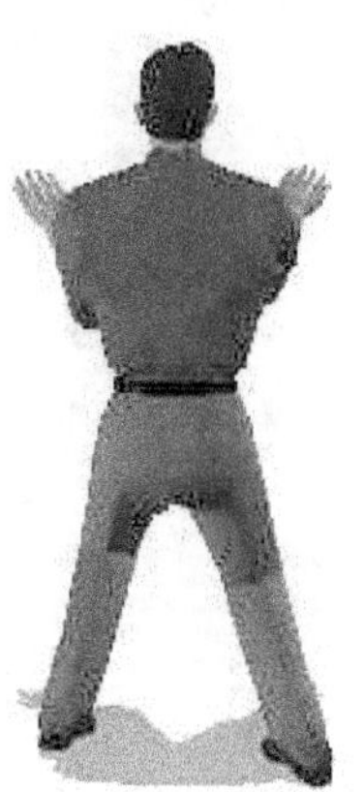

6a)   Left half-moon step into an hourglass.

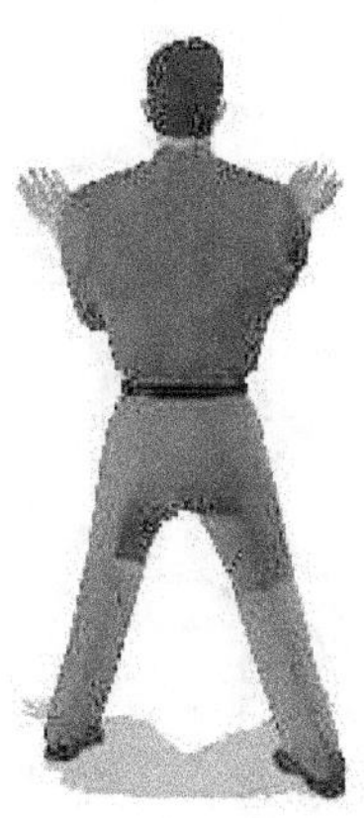

6b)   Execute a right, semi-circular spear thrust. Retract.

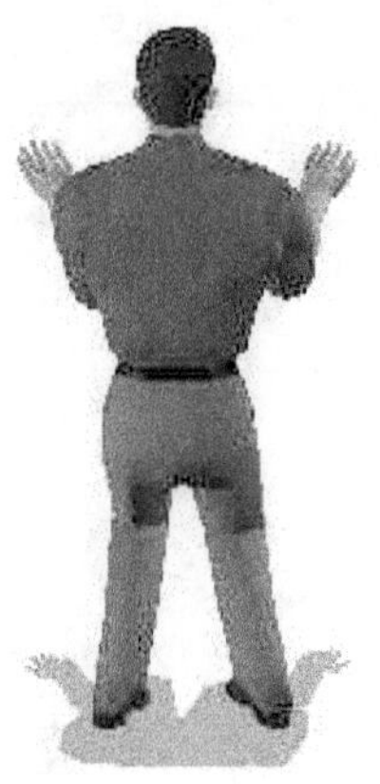

7a)   Right half-moon step into an hourglass stance.

7b)   Execute a left, semi-circular spear thrust. Retract.

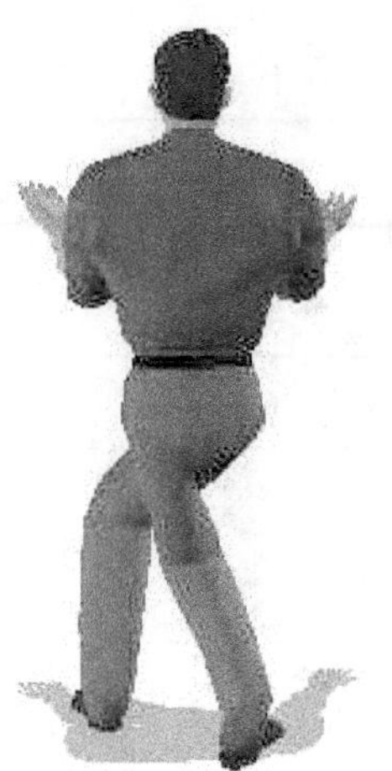

8a)   Right foot steps over the left in a dragon stance. Pivot to face front.

8b)   Execute a right semi-circular spear thrust. Retract.

9a)   Right half-moon step into an hourglass stance.

9b) Execute a left semi-circular spear thrust. Retract.

10a)   Double Spear to the front. Close the fists and pull back as if pulling a great weight.

10b)   Double Spear to the front. Close the fists and pull back as if pulling a great weight.

10c)   Double Spear to the front. Close the fists and pull back as if pulling a great weight.

11)   Step back with the right foot to the right with your left foot into an hourglass stance. The fingers should point into the technique, then snap the right hand into a downward palm block and the left hand into a cross body palm block.

Circle the arms clockwise. Continue the circle until the arms are horizontal.

Retract the arms so that the right is cocked, fingers down, at your hip, and the left is cocked, fingers up, by your shoulder. The elbows should be tight. Push forward with tiger claws.

12)   Step back and to the right with the left foot and back and left with the right foot into an hourglass stance. Snap the left hand into a downward palm block and the right hand into a cross body palm block.

Circle the arms counterclockwise until they are horizontal then pull them back so the left hand is cocked at the hip with the fingers down, and the right hand is cocked at the shoulder with the fingers up. Push forward with tiger claws.

12)	Step back and to the right with the right foot and to the left with the left foot into an hourglass stance. Snap the right hand into a downward palm block and the left hand into a cross body palm block.

Circle the arms clockwise until they are horizontal then pull them back so
the right hand is cocked at the hip with the fingers down, and the left
hand is cocked at the shoulder with the fingers up. Push forward with
tiger claws.

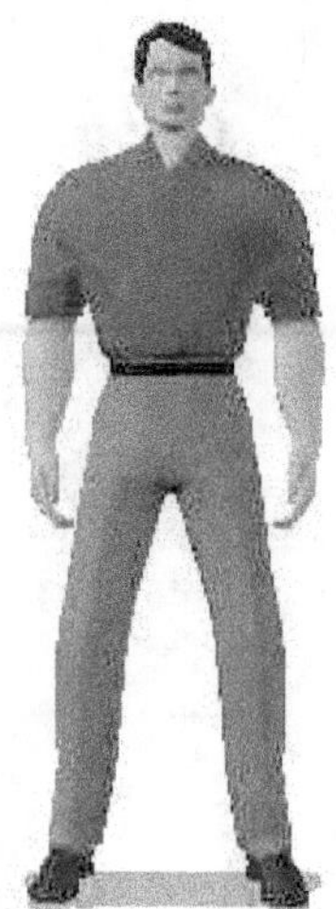

End of form: Retract the right foot to the starting position of the form--relaxed, but ready to move in any direction quickly and easily.

CHAPTER FIVE
THE THREE BATTLES OF SANCHIN
if you don't know sanchin you don't know karate.

A fellow once told me this, and I scoffed. After all, I had over twenty years of studying Karate, how could I not know Karate? Then I learned Sanchin, and found that he was absolutely right.

Sanchin is the heart of the system known as Pan Gai Noon. Pan Gai Noon became Uechi-Ryu, and Sanchin remained the heart. And many different systems of Karate have included Sanchin in their curriculum.

The word Sanchin translates as 'Three Battles,' or 'Three Conflicts.' As with so many words that have made the journey from Founder to beginner over generations and translations, precise meanings are sometimes hard to come by. But it is helpful to examine Sanchin, and Karate, through this concept of 'Three Battles.' There is the obvious meaning of 'Body, mind and soul.' One must train the body to train the mind to train the soul. There are the three elements that one should concentrate on to master Karate: speed, strength and technique. Of course if one wants to really plummet the depths of Sanchin one should consider the three basic geometries within Sanchin.

THRUSTING

Thrusting is the extension of the arms, utilizing the explosion of Tan Tien, as braced by the immovable Hourglass Stance. Within the Kata there are two precise examples of this Thrusting motion. One is the very beginning, one is near the end.

In the beginning example the wrists are raised to the Tan Tien, similar to a gunfighter pulling guns out of holsters, then the spear hands are thrust forward and down.

Original time for learning this Form was two to three years. It wasn't uncommon for a student to do nothing but this downward Spear Thrusting for several months. The reason this opening technique was so important was because it taught the student to put 'Gravity' into his strike. This is to say that the downward sinking of the body didn't even have to be emphasized to get a student to drop his weight and make his Tan Tien work. The direction of the strike increased Gravity without the teacher having to say anything. I call this particular strike the 'Leather Piercer,' and I tell my students they must practice this until they can thrust their fingers through a piece of stretched leather. I also have them practice finger tip push ups, working the fingers the finger as straight, and not claws. And, of course one could return to the original methods of thrusting the fingers into a vat of sand, exchanging the sand for harder materials as time goes by.

HORIZONTAL CIRCLE

The bulk of Sanchin is taken up by the action of stepping while holding the hands as if holding a thousand pound pot. One hand is then circled in, as if blocking, and then thrust outward in a spear.

Walking while holding the pot obviously increases strength. The strike, interestingly enough, is always done wrong. The technique within this motion is a simple Inward Block with the edge of the hand (chop) and then circling the hand to a spear. But most of the people that I have seen do this move execute a straight outward and straight backward motion. Thus the block is obscured and the speed and strength of the action is reduced.

Consider, if you thrust the hand straight out and then pull it back the only muscles that receive work are the forward back muscles. This means that one has to start the arm forward, stop it when it reaches it's destination, then start the arm back, and stop it when it has returned. This is two cycles of start and stop.

But if you circle the arm inward, and continue the circle until the arm is out thrust, there is only one cycle of start and stop. Thus there is a very real blocking motion, and it is done faster because there are less mechanical things to do.

The truth of the matter is that if you do this motion as I have described it you will find that your speed increases dramatically. This is a simple concept of less hard angles and more curves.

VERTICAL CIRCLE

The vertical circle comes at the end of the Form. This is the circular motion done with the hands in claws as one learns to step to the rear and then to the sides. When one enters this particular technique they should point the fingers of the hand that is going to block low in the direction of the block, then wave the hand and snap the palm bone into place. The top hand, while very potential, is more of a guard hand. The Vertical Circle of the hands occurs at this point. At the end of the circle the arms are pushed forward as if pushing a thousand pound whatever.

So let's talk about the manifestation of these three motions into actual technique. The Thrusting motion is obvious. It is a strike.

Wrong.

It is the Mother of all All Strikes!

Stand facing your partner and have him execute in even counts a left punch to your belly, a right punch to your belly, a left punch to your forehead, and a right punch to your forehead. He should punch as hard as he can, but barely touch the skin. As he punches to the belly you should punch with the same side hand and 'Override' his punch. As he punches to the forehead take the inside track and, again with the same side hands, punch through his strikes. As your forearms ram over his forearms your Intention will grow stronger. You will become extremely strong in your punch as you learn to punch through the increased resistance of this simultaneous block and strike.

The second technique is from the horizontal circle movement. When the attacker strikes to your chest simply execute a chop with the cross side hand, insert the same side hand to grab, and let the chopping arm circle in and spear to the throat.

The third technique is from the vertical circle movement. When the attacker strikes to your chest simply execute a slap with the same side hand, insert the cross side hand to grab, and let the slapping arm circle to claw the side of the face.

I usually place the thumb right on the side of the neck. The neck is the connector between the computer and the life support system. There are so many pressure points within this conduit of nerve pulse and oxygen and blood that it is almost impossible not to strike something. You may be surprised at how face the attacker drops. I suggest, however, that you not apply any pressure at all to your training partner. Simply, don't break it if you can't fix it.

While training a person on Sanchin I tend to have them work on the three techniques for a while, then we move into combining the horizontal and vertical circles. The horizontal and vertical circles, describe a mathematical x, y, z controlling of the space around a person through basic blocks. What's interesting is that you can combine them into virtually every potential you will ever need.

I have left out the block for the kick at this early level, though one could insert it easily enough by looking to the Palm Bone block of the vertical circle.

Let's look at the four combinations possible to you through these first two blocks.

CLOSE/CLOSE

The Attacker punches with the right hand. The Defender side steps slightly to the left and forward with the left foot into an hourglass Stance and executes a left Palm and a right grab to the wrist. The Attacker punches with the left hand. The Defender side steps to the right and puts the right foot forward in an Hourglass Stance and executes a right Palm and a left grab, and circles a right Claw to the neck. Continue doing this exercise for a long time.

OPEN/OPEN

The attacker punches with the right hand. The Defender side steps slightly to the right and forward with the right foot into an Hourglass Stance and executes a right Chop and a left grab to the wrist. The Attacker punches with the left hand. The Defender side steps to the left and puts the left foot forward in an Hourglass Stance and executes a left Chop and a right grab, and circles a left Spear to the neck. Continue doing this exercise for a long time.

CLOSE/OPEN

The Attacker punches with the right hand. The Defender side steps slightly to the left and forward with the left foot into an hourglass Stance and executes a left Palm and a right grab to the wrist. The Attacker punches with the left hand. The Defender side steps to the left further, maintaining the Hourglass Stance, and executes a left Chop and a right Grab to the wrist, and circles a left Spear to the neck. Continue doing this exercise for a long time.

OPEN/CLOSE

The attacker punches with the right hand. The Defender side steps slightly to the right and forward with the right foot into an Hourglass Stance and executes a right Chop and a left grab to the wrist. The Attacker punches with the left hand. The Defender side steps further to the right, maintaining an Hourglass Stance and executes a right Palm and a left grab, and circles a right Claw to the neck.

In arranging the two basic blocks of Sanchin in the above four combinations one has not only taken into account virtually every potential of hand strikes, but has also gained some insight as to how to close weaknesses which will arise in the execution of the blocks.

But the real glory in this methodology is that the Instructor does not have to 'Entertain' the student with endless technique. When the student engages upon these four combinations he will rapidly find that his mental no longer works. In one stroke he is cured from that addiction to learning increasing numbers of fancy techniques that don't work, which too many beginners have, and made to understand how to search for true depth of technique which is understandable only through penetrating the fantasy and searching for what works.

CHAPTER SIX
THE BLOCK WALK
'A tight fist is a heavy fist'

While applications can be extracted easily from Sanchin, I prefer to do The Block Walk.

The Block Walk consists of three steps with one person striking low, middle, then high, alternating hands with each strike. The other person steps backward as he blocks low, middle, then high, all with the same hand.

This is an interesting exercise, and you may find yourself having conversations as to which foot is forward, do you strike with the rear hand, etc.

Actually, you can do this with either foot forward, off either the front or rear hand, and as you go back and forth you will find certain patterns evolving. The main thing is not to get confused, but realize that any pattern can work, any stance, and the emphasis here is on just doing it until your arms are tough, and so is your spirit.

This is not a 'do it for a while and move on' exercise; this is a do it for the rest of your life exercise.

THE BLOCK WALK

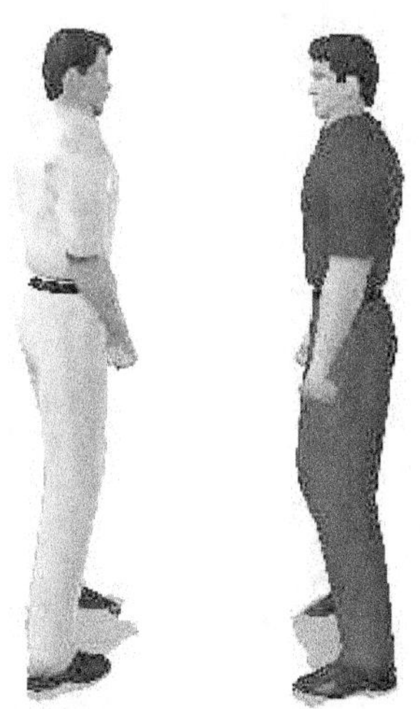

To start: White faces Black.

Step one: Black punches low. White executes a low block.

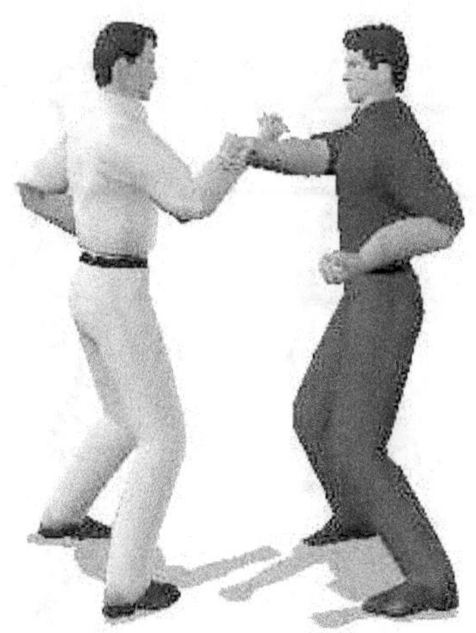

Step two: Black punches middle. White executes an outward middle block.

Step three: Black punches high. White executes a high block with the same hand.

Repeat the three steps, taking turns as attacker and defender.

CHAPTER SEVEN
THE END OF THE ART

One of the first stories I came across was of the old man beating a crowd of bullies using just two fingers. For those interested in such myths let me suggest 'Secrets of Shaolin Temple Boxing,' by Robert W. Smith. And for those of you who wish to attain such skill let me offer you the following knowledge. The Martial Arts are dedicated to: Analyzing and handling Force and Direction (Flow)

And the way to apply this datum is: If the Force is greater Flow it, If the Flow is greater Force it.

And the way to be an old man who can handle the Bully Boys with two fingers is to 'Look.' 'Look,' according to the dictionary means: To see with the eyes. And, later in the definition, to focus attention on.

The fellow outside the Art 'Looks' at the Art and says, 'Gee, I'd like to do that.' The beginner 'Looks' at basics. Tries to figure out which leg to stand on, which move to do, how to breath, and so on. The Intermediate student 'Looks' at Forms, tries to figure them out, tries to cut reaction time, that sort of thing. The Advanced student 'Looks' at combat, tries to figure out how to apply the theory of Form to the chaos of combat, and so on. The Expert student 'Looks' at himself, tries to refine the Art, eliminate excess actions, polish thought, make logical sense out of the mass of data he has acquired. The Master 'Looks' at others. He is aware that he is not the only one in the universe. He appreciates his fellow man, and life is play. The Wizard 'Looks' at others 'Looking.' Concepts have broken free of language, and he is aware of communication far beyond the silly, linguistic type that earthlings use.

'Look.' To perceive with the eyes. But not just with the eyes. Ever feel somebody walk behind you? Feel the 'Radar' in your back charting distance and motion? That's 'Looking,' too. A Martial Artist has several ways of 'Looking' inherent within the confines of the Art. Let me outline another sequence of 'Looking' for you.

The fellow just starting the Art 'Looks' at other bodies moving. Something there...something there... After one month he is 'Looking' at his fist. By placing it on another's body you can 'Feel' inside that body. Where are the bones? Where are the muscles? Where are the tendons? Where are the organs. This particular 'Looking' will continue for as long as the Artist practices the Art, and the sharpness of 'Vision' will be multiplied and enhanced like an inch cut into infinity. But let's continue with specifics in this type of 'Looking,' so as to chart an Artist's progress, over the years, and to give you an idea of where you are and where you might be going.

After a year the Artist might be looking at the snap of tension within his body as he learns to align body parts. After two years he might be 'Looking' at tightening only his fist. After three years he might be 'Looking' at not tightening his fist, but extending the stick of his bones (arm) through the watermelon (body) of his opponent. Intention. Polish. And so on.

Okay, here's another type of 'Looking' that, in some form, will occur, especially if you are in the Grab Arts. 'Look' at the hand that is grabbing you. After a year you might 'Look' at the elbows as cranks to be turned. After two years you might be 'Looking' at the shoulders as something to be unbalanced. After three years you might be 'Looking' at the axis (the line running between the North and the South poles of the body) as something to be under or overturned, tilted, etc.

This brings us to an interesting point. First, you 'Look' at your body. Make connection from Tan Tien to fist, spine to balance, weight between the base of your feet, and so on. When you reach a certain point you begin to 'Look' outwards (from introversion to extroversion). Not only does the Art demand it, in order to be a functioning Art, but part and parcel of playing at being both Attacker and Defender forces you to 'Look' both ways. Remember 'Feeling' with the fist? But thus far we have only extended 'Looking' from the point of view of one body. The Martial Artist will do this until he has sufficient sense of body that the body will begin to move as one unit (I call this CBMing, achieving Coordinated Body Motion). To move beyond this you move into the world of the other person. An insane person will not be able to do this. Because a person cannot do this does not mean he is insane. It's a matter of being able to 'Look,' and to use one's own peculiar abilities to do this.

Though anybody can be an Artist, not all choose to.

So, you 'Look' into the other person's body. In the hard Arts we 'Feel' with the fist. In the soft Arts we 'Feel' directly of the other person's body. Both are right, and both are halves of a whole.

If you do only the hard arts and never the soft your ability to 'Look' deeply will be curtailed at a certain point. If you 'Look' only with the soft Arts it will take too long, because you haven't achieved a proper appreciation for the fist. So you 'Look' with the hard until you CBM. Then you 'Look' with the soft. You 'Look' through the grab, up the arm, through the joints into the body.

Question. Who drives the body?

The answer is to be had by doing technique until you 'See' the Thought Behind the Action.

Can you 'See' the Thought behind your Action? When you CBM you manifest Intention, and you may well be able to track the Intention back to the source.

Can you 'See' the Thought Behind somebody else's Action? If you have CBMed and continue to practice you will be able to. Just find somebody else's Intention and track it back. Sincere practice in the Art of divesting yourself of violence will lead you to this. No violence creates no static of thought creates space through which perceptions flow freely without distortion.

Polishing is the fact of training yourself not to flinch, jerk, twitch or otherwise reaction in the face of incoming Force or Flow. Polishing is the creation of space, first through technique and form, then in Thought. Thus, through Polishing you can see the Thought Behind all Actions. Polishing is training yourself not to 'React,' but to move of your own determination without pattern except as prescribed by incoming Force/ Flow. If you have abberated the Art into a seeking for violence you will never understand this. At least not this lifetime.

So you have an old man. Or a young man who has understood what I have said. Eyes open, 'Looking,' sight not dimmed by threat of violence. Perception outward, utilizing more systems than merely 'Eyes' to 'Look.'

Threat.

Chart Flow so no Force can be created from impact.

Keep body distance appropriate.

If Force does manage to impact upon you simply direct Energy into body part struck.

Concentrate Energy until it feels as solid as matter. Fist bounces off a body integrated in such a manner. CBM carried to logical conclusion will enable you to have such an ability.

But they only strike you if you allow it.

Normally the Art is defined in small slices of inches, and you, by 'Looking' hard and long, control such infinitesimal pieces of the Art.

Fist miss. Slight pull on sleeve, up arm, unbalance axis, attacker falls. Or slight touch with a fist that can 'See' where it is going. Intention between ribs, into organ, wave of Energy, Attacker falls.

Mystical? Nah. Just hard work over time with empty hands developing harmony of spirit that...get the idea?

But you can't just do robotically. You have to 'Look.' If you 'Look' you will see, and thus become 'Aware.' And thus is perception and ability born.

You don't believe me? Believe me. Three decades and it's happening for me. Not all the time, but with enough empirical bent that I know it is true, and enough logical thought behind it so that I can transmit it to you.

Three decades, but you don't have to wait so long. Understand what I am saying, hang this article somewhere and read it every day. And do your forms, go to class, make your progressions through the stages of 'Look' that I have described.

'Look' and you will be aware.

'Look....'

Part Two
SEISAN

introduction
THERE ARE THREE LEVELS TO THE ART

On the first level one studies mechanics, what the structure of the body is, how the muscles work, that sort of thing.

On the second level one studies physics, how energy flows through the body, how to make that energy and how to use that energy.

On the third level one accomplishes the intuitions and advanced perceptions of the arts.

Previously, one would have to study for twenty years or more to understand these levels, and then the understanding would be limited. Through matrixing, however, a person can progress through the three levels within a couple of years. This is because matrixing aligns the data, makes the whole art logical, and reduces it to simple, gradient steps.

Imagine an art with nothing hidden, no mysteries--this is matrixing.

NOTE: Al Case Monkey Boxing is the world's first and only completely matrixed art!

CHAPTER EIGHT
MAKING INTERNAL ENERGY WORK

There are ways to make oneself strong. One could take steroids, pound telephone poles with the bare hands, hang weights from the testicles, and so on and so on. Of course, there are certain drawbacks to some of these methods, to say the least. Interestingly, Internal Energy is much simpler than you might have believed. The trick is to understand the concept, and what that concept feels like inside the body when it is put into action.

Internal refers to being on the inside, such as the inside of the body. Energy refers to the Capacity for Work. So Internal Energy is the capacity for work on the inside of the body. But how do you 'Work' inside the body? After all, we are not talking about muscles, exactly, and you can't lift weights with the liver, so what are we talking about?

In a recent article I referred to Chi (Ki) as a moving mass of Energy. This is the concept we are after here. To gain Internal Energy one must be able to move masses of Energy on the inside of the body. When one moves a mass of Energy to a body part that body part feels denser, more impervious. When one, for instance, gets struck in the body, if one can move a mass of Energy into the area being struck, that area feels more solid, and can resist the strike easier. And when one executes a strike, if they can move a mass of Energy into that strike, the strike will be faster, more solid, more telling.

Now, truth be known, if you do your Forms they can lead you to this ability to move masses Energy around inside your body. However, because Forms are done so poorly, and with such little understanding of CBM (Coordinated Body Motion-when all parts of the body support one Intention) this ability is not often reached, and when it is reached it is not understood except in mystical terms, and it can rarely be developed further.

So, first step, analyze your Forms in concert with the concept of CBM. When your Form is aligned your Intention can manifest, and Internal Energy will be one of the results.

Second, practice some of the following techniques for developing and understanding Internal Energy. These techniques are not harmful, but I would be careful in deviating from them.

BODY TESTING

Do a Front Punch out of a Front Stance. Have somebody push on your fist. If any part of your body is unaligned you will find that the body will suffer what I call 'Form Breaks' under the tension.

Have somebody push on your body through all of your Forms and techniques. If your body cannot conduct the Energy through to the ground then you are doing something wrong and you need to relook at what you are doing.

The point to achieve here is relaxation while doing this exercise. If you are pushing back to hold your ground then you are not doing it right. You need to relax (but not limply) and let the Energy travel through your body. When you can do this effortlessly you are doing the Art correctly. (At this point CBM is merely a matter of timing the correct alignment.)

THE UNBENDABLE ARM

One of the most important concepts in Internal Arts is that of the Unbendable arm. Simply place your arm on somebody's shoulder, elbow pointed down, and have them press downward on the inside of the elbow. By taking a firm stance and breathing into the Tan Tien you increase your Energy, and you can direct that mass of Energy into and through the arm. Done correctly and no one can bend your arm.

THE UNBREAKABLE CIRCLE

You can put masses of Energy into virtually any body part. The idea is to learn to relax the body part sufficiently so that energy can pass through it.

One of the best body parts for understanding this concept is the finger/thumb circle. Simply touch your index finger and thumb and have somebody pull them apart. The trick here is imagine a glowing circle in the hand, and thus to activate all portions of the circle being created. This is a great party trick, if you're into such things, and you can, by simply tracing a circle on the fist of the person trying to learn it, make a person instantly capable of 'Magical Chi Tricks.'

One thing I should mention here is the importance of the Intention in all of this. Sit down, close your eyes, and become aware of your foot. Your foot is now possessed of Chi. It is weak chi, the trick is to make it strong chi. Have somebody push on it and it will push back. The more this is done the more 'Pushingness,' and therefore the more Chi, is going to be in the foot. Get enough chi in that foot and it becomes...more real. Certainly more real than the chest it impacts with in a fight.

It is not just the mass of Energy that is Chi that is important. It is the awareness put into the foot that makes you think it is more real than somebody else might think it. So when somebody pushes on your stance, or tries to open the circle of your fingers, or whatever, they are helping you make something more real. The stronger your Intention the more real what you do is and becomes. Whether you drive a truck or push Chi through your veins, increasing your Intention is the key.

Of course who wants to sit around and be aware of their foot? That is one of the drawbacks of meditation. What good is awareness unless it can be used?

A Form is sometimes called moving meditation. Unless you plumb the Form for applications, and body test it for correct resistance, the Form is useless. It is a pose with no working value. At any rate, if you end up using overt muscle to resist you are doing it wrong. Muscle is not necessarily 'Mind.'

So, you CBM your Form, you practice body testing and applications, and develop simple exercises aimed at strengthening body parts, what's next?

What's next is to explore the exact sensation of Internal Energy as it manifests.

THE WATER METHOD

One of my favorite methods is to tell a student to dip his hands in water and then to 'Flick' them dry with technique. While this is a cheap way to illustrate focus, it goes a long way towards getting a person to manifest Energy.

While we are talking Internal Energy here, one should be aware that visualizing the geometry of a technique into infinity will increase all abilities and energies.

Incidentally, make sure you don't hyper extend any joints by 'over focusing.'

THE SAND PIPE VISUALIZATION

Take a pipe and fill it half with sand. Now, give the pipe one shake and try to get the sand to hit one side of the pipe as a single mass. This is the sensation you are trying to get inside your arms when executing block or strike. The sand is the moving mass of Energy, and the pipe is the arm (limb) through which it moves.

What we are talking about is increasing the 'Weight' of your mind Intention). After all, there is no sand inside your arm. But there is sensation. Certain muscles will react, but the real process here is using that sensation to increase your belief, and as belief increases Intention increases...and Energy (which is quite real, regardless of 'Visibility') increases and is manipulatable.

MORE SAND

Your whole body is a pipe, and you can get the 'Sand effect' of moving masses of Energy through your body by hard and fast shifts of weight. The action of a Form, specifically of concentrating on which leg you are standing on, and shifting the weight of the body into a particular leg in a stance, accomplishes this 'Sand effect' quite well and naturally.

Some Forms are quite deliberately set up to enhance this. However, if you wish to increase this effect dramatically, and to enter the worlds and methods of specific Internal Arts, try moving the sand around inside the body and then whipping it out the arm. This is difficult, and yet simple. It is difficult without seeing it. But it is simple once you understand the motion of the body, and the concept of real weight inherent in the Sand Method. To help you get this concept try the following exercise.

1) Stand in a Natural Stance and shift the sand (weight) to the right leg.   2) Shift to the left leg but put the sand in the left hip.

3) Shift to the right leg but put the sand in the right shoulder.

4) Shift to the left leg but run the sand across the shoulders and down the left arm to whatever block is natural (use the water method, if you wish, to help this last step).

In this exercise you can adjust your body to fit whatever block you happen to be working on. The idea is to bounce your Intention back and forth inside your body, increasing it with each 'Bounce,' until you can 'Fling' it out your arm. You can develop an astounding amount of Energy if you apply this concept to your Classical Forms. As I said earlier, some of your Forms have been quite precisely set up for the development of Internal Energy.

In closing let me say that I was always mystified by certain explanations of Internal Energy detailed by Artists of certain Internal Arts. In the end I found that the Internal Energy I had developed through my studies of Karate was the same as theirs, the only differences being in geometries and angles of body and motion. The confusing thing was in descriptions, which usually weren't clear because of poor understanding of English, inadequate translations, certain idiosyncrasies specific to the manifestation of certain Arts, and so on. This article, if read carefully, should go a long way towards clearing this up.

CHAPTER NINE
THE ANATOMY OF A PUNCH

The extreme philosophy of Karate is: one strike, and the fight is over.

This philosophy has, unfortunately, fallen on hard times. People point to the punishment a boxer takes, the failure of striking arts in the octagon, the amount of punishment a human body can take, and claim that this philosophy is nothing but a myth.

But the one punch win is not a myth; it has just not been properly developed in modern martial arts.

I want you to consider something. I want you to consider that any knock out is accomplished by one punch.

What goes before the one punch is set up, exhausting the opponent, angling for strategy, and so on. But only one punch ever knocks anybody out. The secret is to study this concept until it becomes real and workable in your art. The secret is analyze the concepts of fighting until you don't have to wear a person down until he becomes incapable of mounting sufficient defense to protect himself from the one punch.

That being said, the purpose of this article is to analyze one concept, the punch itself. If you can understand the concept, if you can understand the procedure of analysis, then you can apply that method of analysis to other parts of the art. And thus you can apply strategy properly so as to effectively mount the one punch concept at the very beginning of a fight.

The power of a punch does not come from muscles. It does not come from how big you are, or how mean the look on your face. The power of a punch comes, simply, from the amount of energy you are able to transfer from your body to your opponent's body.

Energy, if you regularly peruse your dictionary, is obviously the capacity for work.

And work, if you keep perusing that dictionary, deals with amounts of weight.

So if you want lots of energy, if you want your art to work, then you have to transfer weight to your opponent's frame. Enough weight and your opponent's frame cannot support itself, and will collapse and become non functioning.

Cool.

Consider, if your opponent was laying upon the ground and you dropped weight lifting disks upon him.

The disk is not rigid, it is not muscular, it just is.

If you drop enough weight the body under the weight starts to hurt, and can be damaged.

Can you launch a punch so that it connects like an inanimate object dropped from a height? I used to call this concept 'the dead punch,' and I guarantee that if you develop it you will become a devoted believer of the one punch school.

I should mention, at this point, that 'dead' doesn't refer to making dead the opponent, but rather depriving your punch of animus at impact. Please look up the word animus.

Let's talk about some of the physics involved in manufacturing the 'dead punch.'

I have been accused of saying, in previous articles, that the body must be treated like a machine.

Guilty.

A machine, to be effective, must be bolted down. In the martial arts this is called grounding. This is sinking the weight so as to bolt the body down.

This is the purpose of stances.

So, you are in a stance, and about to launch a punch.

The first step is to push with the legs.

I say legs, but you will have to discover for yourself how much push is necessary in what harmony (and what order) from which leg. This launching of the body describes the first principle of power: thrusting.

The second step is to turn the hips. You don't overturn them, but rather turn them just enough to put the entire weight of your body into the strike. This turning of the hips describes the second principle of power: rotation.

The third step is to throw the arm. To throw the arm one can simply launch a straight line, utilize an arc (as in, but not necessarily dependent upon, the turn of the hips), lift the shoulder and snap it downward, (this creates a momentary waver in the line of the arm which is called a 'pulse,') and so on.

The fourth step is to sink the weight at the point of impact. You must lock the frame downward, utilizing gravity in the afore mentioned stance. This downward dropping of intention creates more work for the legs, which creates more energy for the Tan Tien, which creates more energy for the strike. I sum this particular concept up as:

weight equals work equals energy

This is 'the Energy Formula.'

This sinking of weight describes the third principle of power: gravity.

The fourth step is to be relaxed throughout, and tighten the fist upon impact. The point here is that a relaxed body is much easier to put into motion than a tight body, but the body must be tightened upon impact to be an effective punching tool. (Indeed, some people hold that the entire body must be a fist. They are not incorrect, but this is only one stage.)

A point here: there is some confusion as to how much of the body should be tightened upon impact.

Because of training methods aimed at children, and because of certain truncated developments in modern teaching methods, some people believe that the whole body must be tight.

Well, perhaps in the beginning, but only until the student learns to establish sufficient body alignment.

The point here is that one cannot tighten forever, one simply runs out of body life. And, to be succinct, by tightening only to a certain point, one can learn to relax the body during strike, and become much, much, MUCH more efficient in the manufacture of strike.

Consider, aside from the body being easier to move while relaxed, more energy can course through the body upon strike if it is properly relaxed.

So at a certain point the body should be consciously 'untightened' upon striking, until one is striking whiplike and softly, and yet imparting *more* than the body weight. (This step can be summated as 'focus.')

If you follow what I've just said here, then you realize that I have just said that you can break the rules of the universe.

It is so. To understand this, however, you must understand the whole picture of what I have been saying here.

The component parts of the strike are: stance, thrust, rotation, arm throw, gravity, relaxation (to focus).

But the components of power are: thrust, rotation, gravity.

Focus, while important and powerful, is a particular of karate, and not essential to understanding the whole. Indeed, other arts use other concepts, but do not deviate (except to their detriment) from the three components of power.

And relaxation should be such a component part of your life that I should not even need to mention it here.

Thus you have three principles of power, and if you can synthesize these three principles into one motion through something I call CBM (Coordinated Body Motion-all parts of the body support one intention), then you will realize the true 'Fourth Principle of Power.'

This principle is intention. And this is the principle that will allow you to break the rules of the universe.

I want you to consider something here. I want you to consider that behind every action is a thought. Simply, there is no action without thought.

The manifestation of this thought is not the leg and the hip and the arm, or even the thrust and the rotation and the gravity: it is the intention that is the direct carrier of the thought. Do the martial arts long enough and this will become not only apparent, but the guiding principle of your life, and of all things in your life.

Okay, go back and read up to this point a few dozen times. Think about, understand, and you will be ready to move on to the complete analysis of art necessary to the development of the one punch. Or the one block. Or, in the extreme (dependant upon your ability to reverse flows in all concepts), the one throw.

First, do your form with an attention to which leg is pushing, and how much, and how much harmony is necessary in conjunction with the other leg. Where are the transference of weight points, and thus new points of push? Where does the leg set up for the next push? Where does it fail to set up for the next push? Don't be surprised to discover that your classical forms have mistakes in them.

Second do your form with an attention to which way your hips turn. Do your hips align with the leg and the arm? Do they slam into the motion? Or retract from so as to establish correct body alignment? Where do the hips add power to the move? Where do they fail to add power? Don't be surprised to discover that your classical forms (after you have remade them to conform with the principle of proper leg pushing) need some adjustment.

Third do your form with proper alignment of the arms. Where do the arms pulse? What geometry are you describing? Are you capable of sustaining power upon impact? Are you capable of creating power in the next move? Don't be surprised to find that your classical forms don't always make sense.

Fourth, do your forms while relaxing. Practice tightening the whole body, practice tightening just the fist. Practice setting yourself up for the next move, and for overall strategies of engagement. You may have to adjust the footworks of the forms to make any real sense of them.

Fifth, do your forms and practice sinking your weight. Which leg(s) do you sink on? Can you keep the proper body alignment? Are you setting up for the next move? Can you CBM all your motions?

Sixth, and this is most important, practice the aforesaid principles over and over and over. While you may run out of body life, you will never run out of art. Practicing these principles will establish your entry not into just how to punch, but into the true art.

Thus, the world may again discover true potentials of an art, and of individuals brave enough to enter into that art.

CHAPTER TEN
THE THIRTEEN BATTLES OF SEISAN

Last month we discussed the Three Battles of Sanchin. We also discussed the first four techniques of Seisan, which are the combinations of the vertical and the horizontal circles within Sanchin. That leaves nine techniques within the Form of Seisan. Before we get into these, however, let me make a couple of points concerning the Form Seisan.

The essence of Sanchin is Power.

The essence of Seisan is Technique.

There is ample room for developing further power in Seisan, and this will happen. But the real glory of Seisan relies on the developing of technique.

The Core technique of this Art is the circle. Be it vertical or horizontal, the essence of the Art is manifested by the Circle Block. This Circle Block is called Wa-uke.

Seisan teaches one all the nuances of the Circle Block.

Footwork is an exploration of different angles in which to set your Stance and do the Circle Block.

The Circle Block, in the Form, is followed up by a variety of strikes, and how those strikes can go back into the Circle Block.

The Circle Block can be done in four combinations of clockwise/counterclockwise with various timings.

And so on.

If you matrix the circling block (outward grabbing block) you will understand this. Leaving that simple matrixing to you, let's explore the remaining techniques of Seisan.

TECHNIQUE FIVE-The first move of Seisan is a double ridgehand strike followed by a knee strike. The technique goes like this.

The Attacker pushes to the body.

The Defender executes a double parry and strikes with ridge hands to the temple.

The Defender then grabs the head and pulls it into a knee strike.

The Defender then lifts one arm and pushes on the head to execute an Inverted Insertion Throw.

A quick word on this technique, one can side step a strike while doing this, palm the ears, and find any other number of variations. The central idea, however, is to understand that the head is just a stumpy little lever and can be used to turn the body just like a mate would turn the wheel to steer a ship.

TECHNIQUE SIX-The essence of this technique is to acquaint a student with certain arm manipulations which are a step outside what the student will certainly understand through a long term study of the Art. What follows is a precise description of the technique, but there is not room to go into the possible variations and deviations.

The Attacker punches to the face with the right hand.
The Defender steps slightly to the side and front with the right foot into an Hourglass Stance as he executes a right Inward Block (Chop) and a left Claw to the wrist, then circles the right Claw to the groin.
After slapping (clawing) the groin, the Defender slaps up on the Defender's right elbow, straightening the elbow out and taking further control of the arm.
The Defender turns the Attacker's right hand, which inverts the whole limb, then simply pushes the Attacker away.

TECHNIQUE SEVEN-The essence of this technique is to speed up the mind by forcing the student to move faster to keep up with a triple attack technique. Also, the student is introduced to the concept of closing distance.

The Attacker kicks to the groin with the right foot.
The Defender twists slightly to the left as he executes a right Reverse Low Block. The left hand circles out through a High Block.
The Attacker punches to the face with the left hand.

The Defender twists to the right as he executes a right High Block. The left hand continues the circle outward and around and comes up the center of the body.

The Attacker punches to the face with the right hand.

The Defender twists slightly to the left as he executes a left Circle Block.

The Defender steps forward with the right foot into a Front Stance as he continues the outer circle of the right arm into an upward (vertical) Elbow Strike.

The Defender then places his right arm across the Attacker's shoulder and, by pushing on the arm and the neck, cranks the Attacker down.

TECHNIQUES 8-13 (see chapter nine--'The Core Application.')

There is one technique, but so durned many applications...but to understand the applications one need merely understand the logic. Let me outline the technique first, and then present the logic.

The Attacker executes a right kick to the groin.

The Defender steps slightly to the right into a Crane Stance on the right foot to as he executes a left Hooking Low Block and a right High Block.

The Attacker executes a right punch to the face.

The Defender places the left foot down, slaps with the right hand.

The Defender steps forward with the right foot as he grabs the Attacker's wrist with the left Circle Block hand and executes a right Horizontal Elbow strike.

The Attacker executes a Throw.

It doesn't matter which hand or foot is striking. Using the same logic you used in understanding every potential combination of the Vertical and Horizontal Circles, and using the 'Sped up thought' you experienced from Technique Seven, you will be able to walk through the Attack while handling whatever arm or foot is given you.

The point here is one of closing distance.

Kick to Fist to Knee to Elbow to Throw...this technique of Seisan works.

You see there is not only the logic of handling all potentials of right and left strikes, but of closing, or even opening, distances between oneself and an attacker.

The way you develop more techniques out of this one technique is in the fact that everybody has two sides, and there are three levels to the body. So, execute the technique and then:

LOWER LEVEL

1) Sweep the foot, or

2) Knee the knee (or back of the calf, or whatever)

MID LEVEL

3) Go under the attack arm and arm sweep the attacker over the leg, or

4) Go under the arm and press the elbow against the small of the back and sweep the attacker over the leg.

HIGH LEVEL

5) Go over the attack arm and execute an Insertion (sometimes called a Rotary) Throw, or

6) Go over the attack arm and sweep the Attacker over the leg.

One Technique, but six explicit variations which, if understood, will lead one to complete control of an opponent.

So, it doesn't matter whether the Attacker's right foot is forward, or the left foot, or whatever. It doesn't matter whether the follow up is right hand or left hand, same side of the body or cross side of the body, or anything else. All that matters is that the student practices to the point where wherever he finds himself, no matter what the Martial Problem, he has a solution.

(More on this technique in chapter seven--'The Core Application.')

Before I close let me make one additional point. The last Form in Pan Gai Noon is called Sanseirui. The translation, I believe, means '39.' Well, there won't be an article called 'The Thirty Nine Battles.' The reason is that while Sanseirui does explore other angles and certain oddities of motion, it is more of a demonstration Form than a workable Form. To be explicit, the technique of the Circle Block is taken a little too far, and the essence of the technique enters a watering down process, versus a 'Soul deepening' process.

Also, I find that there are other exercises that will give better information as to how to use the Circle Block, rather than to go into the realm of too much with too little, as regards this technique. This doesn't mean you shouldn't learn it. It just means that after learning Sanchin and Seisan one should be exploring on their own. The logic of those two Forms is that potent and self-enhancing. I hope that this analysis of the some of the potential techniques within these Forms will aid in this process.

CHAPTER ELEVEN
SEISAN

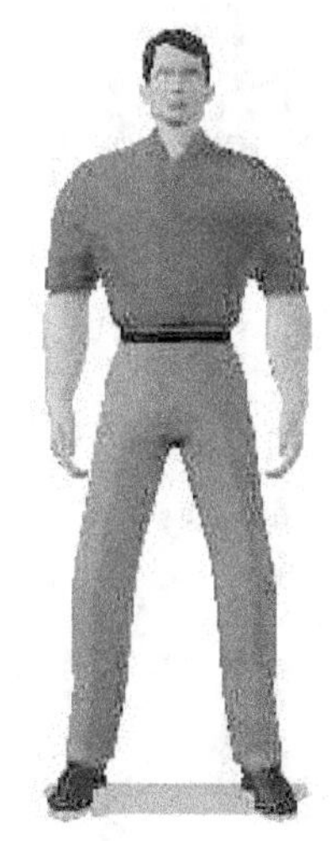

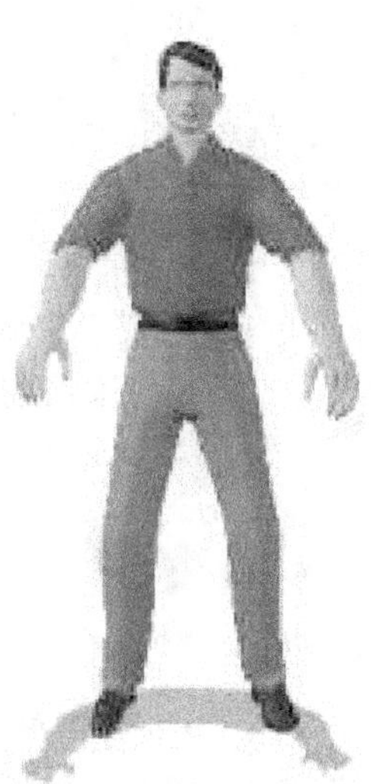

Starting position: relaxed, but ready to move in any direction quickly and easily.

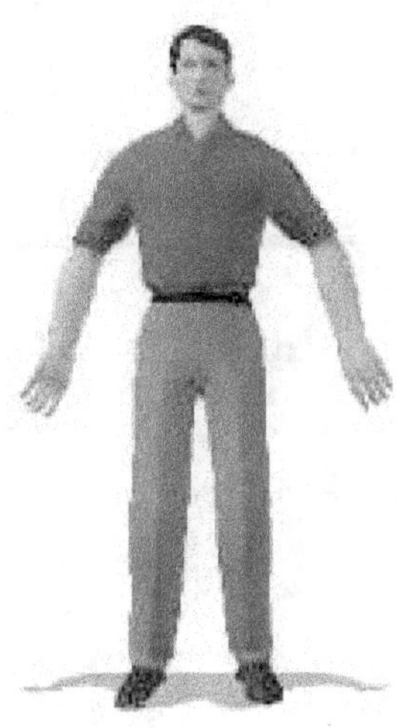

Count 1: Move the right foot in a half moon step into and hourglass stance as you bring the hands out and around through a double parry and execute a double ridge hand strike.

Count 2: Retract the right hand, then pulse a palm strike.

Retract the left hand, then pulse a palm strike.

Retract the right hand, then pulse a palm strike.

Count 3: Raise both hands in a upward beak blocks. Slap the right knee with both hands, then spread the hands out in low blocks.

Place the right foot slightly forward in an hourglass stance as you execute a left low claw to the front and a right low claw to the rear.

Count 4: Pivot to the left, then step across the left foot with the right foot into an hourglass stance facing to the rear (the left foot should be slightly in front) as you execute a left low claw to the front and a right low claw to the rear.

Execute a left outward grabbing block, then take a half moon step to the front with the left foot into an hourglass stance as you execute a right low claw to the front and a left low claw to the rear.

Execute a right outward grabbing block, then take a half moon step to the front with the right foot into an hourglass stance as you execute a left low claw to the front and a right low claw to the rear.

Raise both hands to the waist (as if you were drawing guns from holsters), then shuffle forward with both feet into an hourglass stance (with the left foot forward) as you execute double spear thrusts down and to the front.

Count 5: Close the fists, step back with the right foot and face to the right as you execute a right high block and a left inverted low block.

Keep circling the hands, step forward with the right foot into a front stance as you execute a left outward grabbing block and a right vertical elbow strike (with right beak).

Count 6: Retract the right foot to an hourglass stance as you circle the hands through a left palm block to a right outward grabbing block.

Execute a left palm thrust.

Circle the hands through a left low palm and a right palm block.

Circle the hands to a left outward grabbing block. Execute a right inverted (palm up) spear thrust.

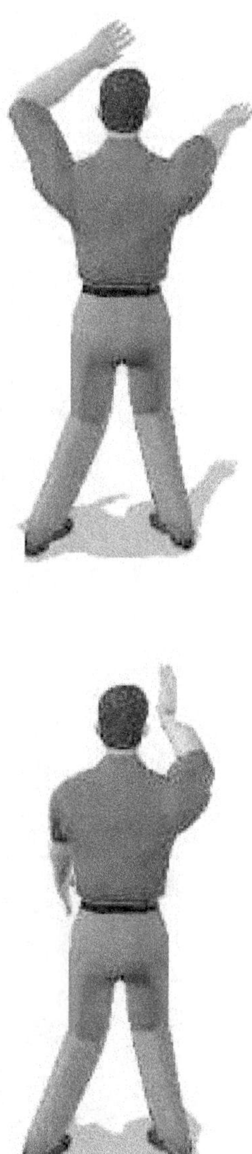

Count 7: Step forward and to the right with the right foot into an hourglass stance facing to the left. Circle the left hand through a block.

Circle the hands to a left outward grabbing block, then raise the right hand up and out.

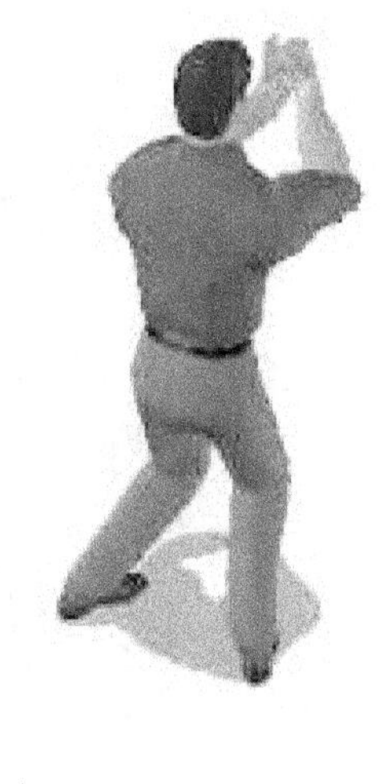

Execute a right hammer to the left palm, then circle the hands to a right outward grabbing block. (The left hand doesn't circle so much as bounce.)

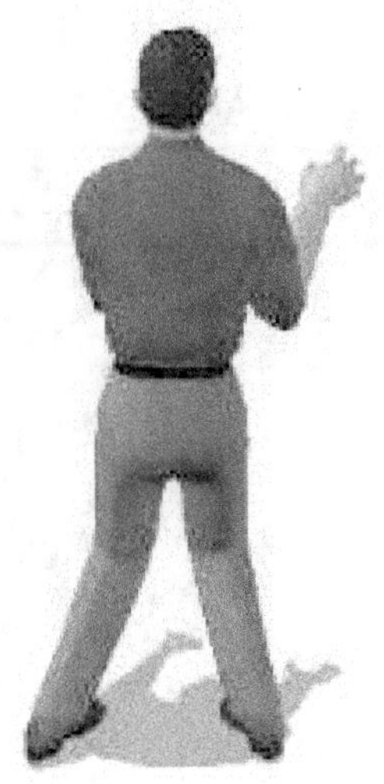

Execute a left outward grabbing block.

Count 8: Step back and to the right with the right foot into an hourglass stance as you circle through a right high block. Circle the right hand down through a low palm and the left hand through a palm block.

Execute a right outward grabbing block. Execute a left inverted (palm up) spear hand.

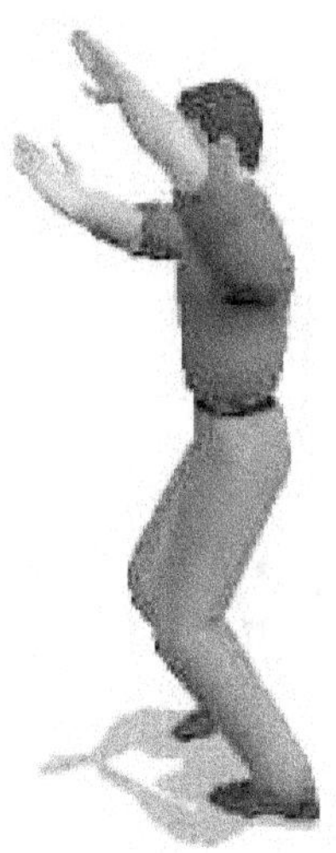

Count 9: Step to the left across the left foot with the right foot into an hourglass stance as you circle through a left high high block. Continue circling the hands through the pole position (right palm block, left low palm block.)

Circle the hands to a left outward grabbing block. Execute a left front locking snap kick.

Execute a right downward punch a left downward punch, a right downward punch, and a left downward punch.

NOTE: The above four strikes should actually be done with the foreknuckles of the hands. My graphics program wouldn't show this.

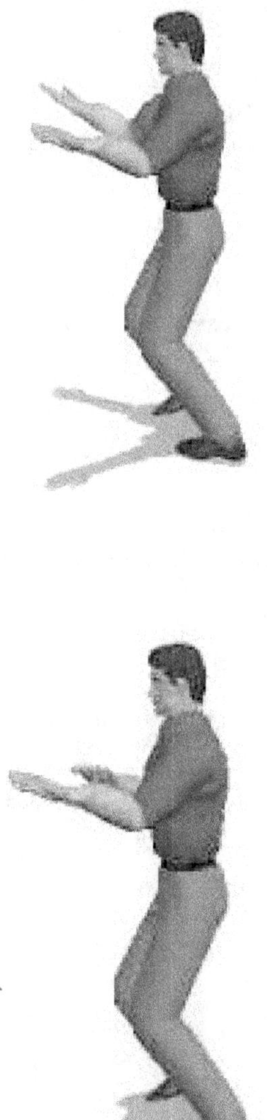

Cross the hands and raise them and open them into two outward blocks.
Bring the right hand in and back in a circle.

Continue the circle to thrust the right hand outward in a curved elbow thrust.

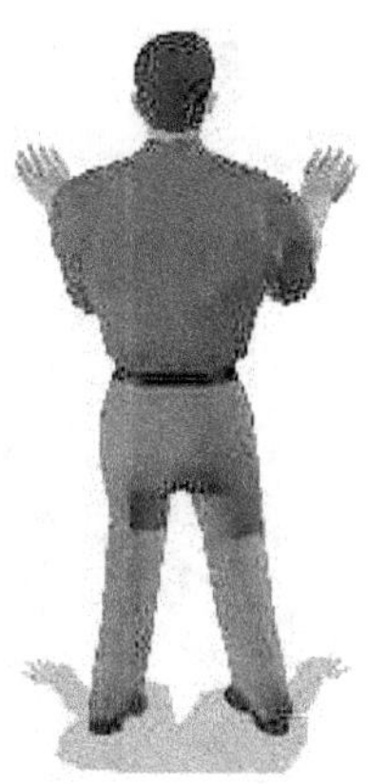

Count 10:   Step back and to the right with the right foot into an hourglass stance. Arms should assume the double outward block positions. Circle the left hand in and back to execute a left curved elbow spear thrust.

Count 11:   Step to the left across the left foot with the right foot into an hourglass stance. Arms should assume the double outward block positions. Circle the right hand in and back to execute a left curved elbow spear thrust. Retract the arm to the outward block position.

Count 12: Circle the right arm up and the left arm down, execute a left outward grabbing block.

Execute a right inverted (palm up) spear thrust.

Step forward in a half-moon step with the right foot as you circle the right arm down and the left arm up. Step out to an hourglass stance as you execute a right outward grabbing block.

Execute a left inverted spear thrust (palm up).
Step forward in a half-moon step as you circle the left arm down and the right arm up.

Step out to an hourglass stance as you execute a left outward grabbing block. Execute a right inverted spear thrust (palm up).

Count 13: Step back with the right foot as you circle the right hand down through a palm block and the left hand up through a palm block. Continue back into a right crane stance as you execute a right high knife and a left low hook.

Step forward with the left foot as you circle the arms inward. Step forward with the right foot into a horse stance as you execute a left outward grabbing block.

Bring the left hand back and around and the right hand back and around and execute a right elbow slap to the left palm.

Execute a left outward grabbing block and circle the right hand over to execute a backfist. Retract the right arm.

Execute a punch with the right foreknuckle.

End of form: Retract the right foot to the starting position of the form--relaxed, but ready to move in any direction quickly and easily.

CHAPTER TWELVE
THE ESSENCE OF PAN GAI NOON

It is hard to nail down the essence of Pan Gai Noon. The name itself means 'Half hard/half soft.' It is based on three animals: Tiger, Crane and Dragon. It is an old system, yet fresh out of Mother China, as far as times in the Martial Arts go. In addition it is called Karate (Uechi-Ryu) in Japan, and has probably undergone some cultural influences.

So what is the essence of this system?

The essence is revealed in a depth of technique which is singular to the system, unique to the system, but which is sometimes hard to discern for the variety and richness of the system. This article will discuss that one technique, and you may be surprised at how understanding this concept will effect and enhance your own Art.

Before I continue, however, I should stress that Pan Gai Noon is different from Uechi-Ryu. The difference is most easily apparent in the number of Forms. Uechi-Ryu practices eight forms. But five of them were designed by the Kanei Uechi. In examining the system I realized that the extra five forms, though interesting and of peripheral value, did not really provide me with any new information concerning the Core Technique of the system. And, in fact, George Mattson, in his wonderful book on Uechi-Ryu, made the statement that Kanei Uechi's purpose in teaching these Kata, originally designed for Demonstrations, was to 'Hold the attention of the modern day, impatient student,' which leads one to believe that the additional five forms are used to entertain the Uechi-ryu practitioner, and keep him interested long enough to truly plumb the depth of the Art. Because of the truth of that statement, which my own 27 years experience in the Martial Arts validated, I chose to intensify my studies of the three Core forms of Pan Gai Noon, rather than allow myself to be sidetracked into other forms which, truth be known, are more rearrangements of the material of the original three forms than anything else. (See pg 94 of 'Uechi Ryu Karate Do,' by George Mattson.)

The Core Technique of Pan Gai Noon can be looked at from any one of the three animals manifested within the system. The Tiger has a Claw. The Dragon has a Claw. And the Crane has a Beak. Each of these hand configurations can be used to grip an opponent. Each of these can be used to follow and control an opponent. And this leads us into that technique which I wish to present as the perfect Pan Gai Noon technique. Following is a breakdown of how that technique develops, and how I relate to it as an Instructor.

1) When I am teaching a beginner I teach them to use the circular motion of the arm as a simple block. Thus they can concentrate on the simplicities of block and defense. During this time the student should be concentrating on Sanchin.

2) As the student becomes Intermediate I encourage them to practice until the simple circular movement can be used to literally grab an Attacker's wrist out of mid air.

During this time I encourage the student to practice several types of counters, and to inspect the second Form Seisan, for variety. I draw on the Form for these counters, for within the forms, connected to that simple (but oh so difficult) grab, are Kicks, Spear Hands, Palm Strikes, Hammers, Claws, Elbows, and so on.

Also, during this time I encourage the student to engage in all manners of multiple strike exercises. The idea is to teach the student to grab, let go in the event of second and third strikes, use both arms in conjunction with each other, and so on.

3) As the student becomes Expert I encourage him to develop the Grab into Throws. Some people don't realize it, but the Horizontal and Vertical Elbow strike lead directly into some incredibly potent Throws that are extremely difficult to guard against. Within the Block, Grab, Throw sequence you will see a progression of closing distances that is very important to appreciate if you are going to understand all the varieties of counters and how to develop them into Throws. During this time the student should practice the Form Sanseirui.

Thus, the Perfect Technique of PGN begins with as a Block.

Develops into a Grab with a variety of potentials.

And ends as a Throw.

Variations can often be woven into Two Man Exercises.

And we haven't even looked at such things as pressure point strikes or weapons disarms.

At this point let me offer a scenario for manifestation of the perfect PGN technique, which will demonstrate how to put all that I've said into a very advanced technique. (see chapter nine--'The Core Application.')

1) Attacker offers a left kick to the groin.

PGN student executes a right Low Block (utilizing the Palm Bone) to

the shin.

2) Attacker offers a right punch to the body.

PGN student executes a left grabbing block which stops but doesn't

catch the Attacker.

3) Attacker offers a left punch to the face.

PGN student sidesteps slightly to the right and passes the Attacker's

left hand with his right hand.

4) PGN student catches the Attacker's left wrist with his left hand.

5) PGN student executes a right Phoenix Eye to the Attacker's ribs.

6) PGN student executes a right Horizontal Elbow to the Attacker's

head.

7) PGN student steps behind the Attacker's left leg with his right leg

and pushes the Attacker back over his leg with his right arm, thus

Throwing him.

Let me give you another scenario, so you can see how to develop a Throw on the other side of the body.

1) The Attacker offers a left kick to the groin.
The PGN student executes a right Low Block (Utilizing the Palm
Bone) to the shin.
2) The Attacker punches to the face with the right hand.
The PGN student executes a short left grabbing block and catches the
Attacker's right wrist.
3) The PGN student executes a right Phoenix Eye to the sternum.
4) The PGN student executes a right Horizontal Elbow Strike to the
Attacker's head.
5) The PGN student places his right forearm across the Attacker's neck and uses the neck and the left grab on the Attacker's wrist to execute an Insertion Throw.

I know there are those who claim that sequences such as I have described are too much to do, especially in the event of an Attacker that, contrary to popular demonstration, is moving fast.

Karate, on the whole, has gotten a bad rap as a 'Non-moving' kind of Art. This is because the Attacker is unusually motionless and compliant during the course of a demonstration.

This, unfortunately, is true for some kinds of Karate, especially the way they are taught today. The solution, the way one revitalizes Karate and finds the originally unbeatable Art, is to examine old training methods. Consider that the three original Forms of Pan Gai Noon were taught over a period of about fourteen years. This can be a very long and intense time to study only three forms and the pieces leading up to the sequences I have described. But I doubt if anybody complained about Karate's 'Lack of mobility' back then.

When training in the old methods, when one trains exclusively on one technique, excluding the fun of exploring varieties that may not be all that effective, the Art of PGN will begin to manifest, and that Art, as any other Art of competence, will not depend upon compliant Attackers. Any good Art, practiced intently without distraction, will give to the student the essence of that Art. And that essence may be quite different than the endless Forms that surround it. The trick is to separate the useless from the essence.

In closing let me ask you...is there a Core Technique in your system? Is there a specific technique which you can explore to a depth of degree such as the one I have described here? If there isn't then there are one of two things you can do.

1) You can change systems.

2) You can study deeper and harder, using old training methods, and giving up the 'Fast food' approach to the Martial Arts.

Which advice you follow is up to you. Have a good skill.

CHAPTER THIRTEEN
THE CORE APPLICATION

There are three concepts here:

A Core Application is that application which sums up the major point of a form.

A Universal Application is one which can be worked on two sides. (left or right, open or close, etc.)

An Infinite Application is one which can be worked on 'eight sides.'

Well, there aren't eight sides to a body, unless one considers both sides of the right leg, both sides of the left leg, both sides of the right arm, and both sides of the left arm.

Here's the trick: one must be able to handle any limb from either side, and travel through any follow up attacking limbs, on either side, until the opponent is pretzeled.

If you can identify the essential technique of a form, that technique which seems to sum up the form, work, then you are doing a Core Application.

If you can make that technique work on both sides, then you are doing a Universal Application.

But if you can make that technique work on either side of whichever limb he throws, and you can still make it work on either side of any follow up attack, and it doesn't matter how many follow up attacks he throws, you can still make it work, well, then, you are doing an Infinite Application.

THE CORE APPLICATION

To start: White faces Black.

Step one: Black kicks. White cranes and executes a left low (hooking) block.

Step two: Black punches. White steps down with the left leg and forward with the right leg into a horse stance as he executes a right palm block
Step three: White pulls black's arm with the left hand and executes a right horizontal elbow strike.

Step four: White extends his right arm next to Black's neck, then moves forward, pushing the neck down and around, and Black's right arm up and around.

The result is called a vertical armpin.

Can you make this technique work, hook kick on either side, slap punch on either side, grab art of some sort on either side? One should always attempt to understand a Core Application until it is an Infinite Application.

CHAPTER FOURTEEN
SINGLE FINGER KARATE

It has become a common belief, in recent times, that stand up fighting is inadequate. In particular, the Ultimate Fighting Championships have proven this. Stand up fighter after stand up fighter have gone to the mat and been choked out or forced to submit, and one of the Arts most associated with this 'Stand Up Inability' is Karate.

And Ju Jitsu has been proven to be the best Art. Right?

Wrong.

All the UFC has proven is that we, in America, don't know how to do Karate.

I know the truth of this statement for a very simple reason: I was there when Karate went bad in this country.

Furthermore, I can help you understand what went wrong, why Karate is not a bad Art, but a superior Art, and how you can make your particular style of Karate into something that is quite ferocious.

I began my study of Karate in 1967. It was touted as the Art by which even a woman or child could subdue a grown man.

Schools were springing up on every block, Bruce Lee would hit the tube shortly, and the so called 'Golden Age' of Karate, and the Martial Arts in general, would occur.

Actually, the Golden Age did not occur; marketing occurred, and the Arts spread across the country so fast that all that was offered the public was a hollow shell.

The first school I entered, there were less than twenty schools in the SF-Bay Area at the time, apprised me that this technique would result in instant death, so I shouldn't use it. And this technique would maim my opponent in quick snap time, so I should be very careful when I walked the streets. And this technique....

Get the idea? I was told I was dangerous and, being gullible, I believed it.

The first time I had to use my Art it failed.

So I went to another school, and the sad facts of reality were finally introduced to my suburban cranium.

The Art is not a marketing ploy, it is real, and it will work--BUT IT MUST BE MADE TO WORK!

How do you make an Art work?

Before I answer this question let me make a point: during those times I knew people that could do real, emphasize 'REAL,' Karate. I knew people who could put a Single Finger through a hanging one inch pine board.

Where are those people now? What happened to the people who knew the Real and True Art?

We see all the 'Masters' selling their wares in the mags, but how many of those Martial Superstars can do such a trick?

The fact is that those types of Martial Artists were starting to be grown in America, but marketing happened, and the growing stopped-- and a large, unique field of knowledge has been lost.

People are now more concerned with winning the tournament, doing the flashy back flip, having a chain of schools, and the True Art is not in existence in America.

(Lest you think America is alone in this degradation--in 1950 there were supposed to be over 50 people in Taiwan who could perform tricks of the 'Single Finger' nature. These people had fled communism, and the resulting government control of Martial Arts, for freedom. Now, sad to say, there are virtually no 'Single Finger' Artists in Taiwan.)

It should be obvious that a Single Finger Artist would fare well in today's modern extreme fighting, but, as far as I know, there are no contestants in the Extreme Arena that can break a board using but a Single Finger.

I have spoken at length concerning this matter of being able to use one finger, and the reader should know that I have chosen this ability merely to describe a higher level of Art. There are many other abilities inherent within a study of the True Art, should one be fortunate enough to find an example of the True Art.

But, as I have indicated, there are virtually no schools, in the United States today, which teach a level of Art associated with the 'Single Finger.'

Okay, that Art is lost.

So, how do we regrow it?

We regrow it from the ground up.

If you re-evaluate your Art from the ground up, from Stances, you will find the strength necessary to create the ability to use One Finger. Interestingly, once that strength starts to occur you will find yourself 'drawn forward' by the Art, and you will need no extra instruction to break boards with a Single Finger, or do other tricks of similar high nature.

To continue: the purpose of Stance is to create a motor.

A motor is a device that transforms Energy into Work.

Think about that when you are being told that you must bounce and shuffle so as to avoid that incoming punch.

Bounce and shuffle is boxing, and that is a fine sport.

But Karate is an Art, and the point of Karate is that by holding your ground you can create a motor, which motor will create the Energy necessary to break the incoming punch. Or to break a board with a Single Finger.

Of course, if you practice with gloves on it is difficult to get this idea. The hands being bound inhibits the Artist's ability to Focus Energy.

This concept of a motor is a rather interesting one. Simply, by holding two terminals apart, two terminals that wish to come together, tremendous energy can be built. The terminals in this case are the legs. The terminals lead to the Tan Tien, and the Energy is redirected from that point depending upon what task you have set yourself.

And the longer one holds the terminals apart, the more pain one endures, the more Energy one will have.

Notice that the first thing a grappling stylist does is try to break his opponent's connection with the ground.

And Karate-ists, not yet mature in their Art, fall to defeat and think that their Art will never work, and they go to boxing, or wrestling, or some other sport.

But if the Karate-ist would make up his mind that he just needs to work harder to make his Art work, then the motor would have a chance of starting, and his Art would have a chance of glowing.

Gichin Funakoshi practiced his stance by standing on his roof with a tatami mat in hand during a hurricane.

My instructor had a wonderful trick: he would sit on a barstool, drink in hand, and ground so effectively that several people could not shove him over.

Now that is a stance!

The trick here is that at a certain point the motor turns on and the student becomes capable of a Tractor Beam. That Tractor Beam goes out from the Tan Tien, down the legs, and grabs onto the planet as effectively as fingers hold an apple. Anybody who has ever heard of the holes ground into the floor of the Shaolin Temple can now understand how those holes came to be. They are not holes, worn into the surface, but rather dents, impacted by weight sinking to create a tractor beam .

When I watch Karate on TV and see fellows with gloves bouncing in a ring I know just how far the Art has fallen. When I see Artists having no Stance with which to fend off the efforts of a grappler I know that the Art is something that never came to fruition on these shores.

The True Art enables the practitioner to perform superhuman feats, and these fellows counting coup in the ring are not performing superhuman feats.

Here's an exercise that is seminal to creating the True Art of Karate: Stand in a Horse Stance, buttocks at a level of the top of the knees, for two hours.

That's right...two hours.

You may want to work up to it.

We used to call this Horse Meditation in my school, and we would a stance while holding a high block with one hand, and extend the other hand to the side and curl the fingers in a beak so that we could stare at the tips of the fingers. The beak would curl to the rear and we would see the fingers over the top of the twisted wrist.

Let me give you a great hint: Concentrate on breathing. Breathing works directly on the Tan Tien, and it tends to create an internal calmness so great that when the pain starts to build the student can withstand it.

There are two points at which a student will quit this exercise. The first point is within a minute or so, when the pain starts to build. The way to get through this point is to realize that you aren't going to die, you are just going to hurt; and you must understand that you will hurt, and that the only way to get through the pain is to make up your mind---and just do it.

If you make it to five minutes you will enter the second stage, and you will come across a far more insidious reason to quit.

Once you have decided to endure the pain, accepted pain as something that won't kill you, and gone to breathing as an alternative, you will start to become detached from your body. This detachment can be simple and slight, just a feeling of being removed, or it can be quite a bit more severe...and frightening.

Whatever the degree of separation you experience you will want to quit the exercise.

It is crucial, at this point, that you don't.

Do not accept any justification. Do not say, 'Oh, I can do this, it's simple, I don't need to do this any longer.'

You must persevere! You must, or the pain you just went through won't mean anything, and the True Art will continue to elude you.

In closing, let me say that Karate has taken it on the chin for many years. Before Ju Jitsu there was Bruce Lee with his 'Classical Mess,' and before that you can bet that idiots everywhere went about trying to prove that their Art was best, and that some other poor fool's Art was not.

And practitioners of Karate have not been immune to this silly business of trying to enhance oneself by putting another's Art down.

But the True Artist has no need to prove his Art best because he has achieved a state of...'Satisfaction.' (For this reason you will probably never see a Single Finger Artist in the Extreme Arena.)

At any rate, I guarantee that if you do Horse Meditation for a couple of hours you will have no interest in putting another's Art down. You will not be possessed of any degree of insecurity, and your own Art will have opened up, and so will horizons so vast that you have no idea, as I write these words, that they even exist. Indeed, you will find that there are a variety of True Arts, and that each Art endows the practitioner with incredible abilities, abilities not rooted in fame and glory and money, but rather in realms unknown by those who 'Tug of war' for a living.

I say this: The Golden Age is in front of us.

Can you work hard enough?

Can you make it happen?

About the Author

Al Case walked into his first martial arts school in 1967. During the Gold Age of Martial Arts he studied such arts as Aikido, Wing Chun, Ton Toi Northern Shaolin, Fut Ga Southern Shaolin, Weapons, Tai Chi Chuan, Pa Kua Chang, and others.

In 1981 he began writing for the martial arts magazines, including Inside Karate, Inside Kung Fu, Black Belt, Masters and Styles, and more.

In 1991 he was asked to write his own column in Inside Karate.

Beginning in 2001 he completed the basic studies of Matrixing, a logic approach to the Martial Arts he had been working on for over 30 years.

2011 he was heavily immersed in creating Neutronics, the science behind the science of Matrixing.

Interested martial artists can avail themselves of his research into Matrixing at MonsterMartialArts.com.

MonsterMartialArts.com

Did you know...

Al Case has written over forty novels?
Go to:

AlCaseBooks.com

Matrixing Kenpo Karate Series!

Pre-Matrixing Series

MARTIAL ARTS BOOKS
On the internet

Advanced Tai Chi Chuan for Real Self Defense!
Black Belt Yoga
Five Martial Arts!
The Last Martial Arts Book (w video links!)
Hidden Techniques of Karate (w video links!)
How to Fix Karate (book one) (w video links!)
How to Fix Karate (book two) (w video links!)
Matrixing Kenpo Karate: Creating a New Kenpo
Matrixing Kenpo Karate: The Real History
Matrixing Kenpo Karate: The Secret of Forms
Neutropia ~ Surrealistic Poetry
The Book of Matrixing
The Book of Neutronics

VIDEO INSTRUCTION
DVDs and downloads at MonsterMartialArts.com

Matrix Karate
Matrix Kung Fu
Matrix Aikido
Master Instructor Course
Shaolin Butterfly
Butterfly Pa Kua Chang
Matrix Tai Chi Chuan
Five Army Tai Chi Chuan
Matrix Tai Chi Chuan
Five Army Tai Chi Chuan
Matrixing Kenjutsu
Blinding Steel (Matrixing Weapons)